pas de deux

Also by Indrani Perera and published by Ginninderra Press
Defenestration

Indrani Perera

pas de deux

for Airlie and Phoebe

pas de deux
ISBN 978 1 76041 832 8

Cover: Indrani Perera

First published 2019 by
GINNINDERRA PRESS
PO Box 3461 Port Adelaide 5015 Australia
www.ginninderrapress.com.au

excavate your truth
word by word
line by line
take my hand
and dance

Contents

I Entrée 11

Summer Alive 13
Creek 14
Oxalis 15
Wing 16
Sweep 17
Shimmer 18
Spinning Free 19
Wednesday Afternoon 20
Symphony 21
Fragments 22
Heartbeat 23
Flight 24
Queen of the Road 25
Drive 26
Umbra 27
Wild 28
One 29
The Bone Bride 30
Every Word 31
Words For Sounds 32
Hear 33

II Adagio 35

Searching 37
Wonder 38
Mother 39
Tender 40
Fierce 41
Daylight Savings 42
Afternoons 43

My Time 44
Dinner Time 45
Bedtime 46
A Friend of Mine 48

III Variation A 49

Burn 51
Ignite 52
Write Me a Poem 53
My Words 54
No thing 56
Waterfall 57
Failure 58
Empty 59
Screw It 60
Instructions For Poets 61
Soul Ink 62
The Shift 63
The Poet's Express 64
Neo Logo 65
Twenty Years 66
The Problem 67
Green Grass 68
Blue 69
Lies 70
But What Does It Mean? 72
This 73
Schroedinger 74
It's All Been Done 75
Fear 76
Muse 77
Directions to the Edge 78

IV Variation B 79
Your Turn 81
Tell Me 82
What Do You Feel 83
And What Do You Hear 84
Most Importantly 85

V Coda 87
The Trick Is 89
Stop Apologising 90
Seekers of the Edge 91
You've Got This 92
Run On 93

Acknowledgements 94

I

Entrée

Summer Alive

sun kissed
skin
sting

wind whipped
hair
blind

rock wrecked
feet
pierced

wave washed
body
wham!

burnt, messy
dirty, salty
breathless
– here

Creek

ripple, plop
bare feet
rock
ouch!

splish, splash
hot skin
water
aaah…

flicker flit
dragonfly
sun in my eye

Oxalis

heart-shaped leaves
bloodstained
nodding yellow bonnets
sour grass

Wing

soot smudges flapping
wheel and glide
dip and spin
hold steady
beat
wind

storm ships scudding
polished stone sky
water drenched land
storm lashing tide

metal monster revving
roar and hum
lean and turn
hold steady
pause
rain

Sweep

shhhhhhk
shhhhhk
shhhhhhk
calls the wind

cold metal bites skin
breeze kisses cheek
hair rises on flesh

swoop and dart
stealthy silent
flying past

inky shape hunts
still wonder
in the dark

Shimmer

a thousand tiny circles of light
dancing on the hanging leaves
of the tree
like tiny embroidered mirrors
on a silk sari
bending light from the rippled surface
of the lake in summer

into a moment of heart's quiet
the pause between breaths
thoughts shine glistening golden rays
deep water
waves

Spinning Free

standing in a circle movement flickers
at the edge of my vision

I look up into the spreading branches
of the river red gum outstretched
against the blue, blue sky

light catches a leaf that whirls and twirls
spins and flies from the tree

breaking from the group she cries
'I'll catch it' and runs towards the leaf
spinning to the ground

Wednesday Afternoon

a yellow leaf
drift falls
caresses earth
lands green
– almost new

lower leafed
branches dance in
dappled light
high in the canopy
the breeze
ruffles leaves
shhhhhhhhhhh

children play
cops and robbers
tea parties and sword fights
they'll sleep well tonight

Symphony

swish swish swish
goes the grass
against my feet

thud thud thud
go my heels
on the dirt

jingle jingle jingle
go the keys
in my pocket

fooo-o fooo-o fooo-o
sing the birds
in the trees

chatter chatter chatter
go the voices
in my head

Fragments

a snowflake melting on a windowpane
touched by wonder

a leaf spiralling down to the ground
blessed by joy

a caterpillar crawling up a tree
filled with awe

a stream running over rocks
wild with magic

delight

Heartbeat

dance in the light between breaths
the space without thought
the moment before talk

move under the sun
between the leaves
in the shade of her walk

feel the heat
drumbeat
heartbeat
dance on

leap into the sound under silence
the joy without fear
the instant of touch

ride on the wind
between the birds
in the light of her joy

hear the song
loud strong
heartbeat
play on

Flight

black masked brown duck
gliding on the murky stream
playing in the shadows of light

sulphur-crested cockatoos
landing in the tree tops
screaming at the top of their lungs

valley in the heart of the soul
hide me
hope in the middle of the night
fear me

red breasted welcome swallows
swooping over the silent lake
chasing all their dreams to come

native noisy miner birds
flying to their hidden nest
frantically feeding their young

river in the dark of the womb
heal me
love in the heat of the day
save me

Queen of the Road

speeding on hot bitumen
windows wound down low
looking for a cool breeze
hoping my dream will show

eagles soaring overhead
trees flickering past
squinting at the bright sun
finding my dream at last

stereo blaring music
shouting above the din
knuckles white on the wheel
praying my dream will end

roadkill on the shoulder
crow pecking the eye
sweat trickling down my spine
waiting for my dream to die

diamonds in the heavens
harvest moon in the sky
breathing in the hot air
longing for another try

Drive

my window's down all the way
right arm leans on the door
left hand easy on the gearstick
my bare feet burn on the pedals
as I change gears

shift gear

I've got the radio turned up
loud
drumming my fingers on the wheel
pounding bass driving through the centre
as I sing at the top of my lungs

sing on

the stench of sunbaked seaweed, midday
and rotting fish, three weeks
fills my nostrils
as I speed through the red light

speed up

the sun burns the skin on my right shoulder
and the sweat runs down my spine
as I lean in to the curve

lean in

Umbra

shadow wolves
running running
running up the hill
black as smoke
from the fiery sky

shadow wolves
snapping snapping
snapping at my heels
silent as night
folded into day

shadow wolves
nipping nipping
nipping at my toes
hungry as ambition
thwarted by desire

shadow wolves
following following
wherever I go

Wild

stone and bone
claw and tooth
blood and truth
hone

One

pack up the sorrow
in carefully folded lines
a crow in flight

The Bone Bride

the bone bride
the devil's plight
walking abroad
this long night

the bone bride
the devil's stride
coming for me
this dark tide

the bone bride
the devil's strife
take me away
from this cold life

Every Word

every word
warbling in the sky
is a bird we teach to sing*

every thought
slithering silently by
is a snake we hope to charm

every deed
dug deep into the earth
is a tree we seek to plant

screech, slither, sway
true, wise or deep
our words, thoughts, deeds
onwards they creep

* *Every word is a bird we teach to sing* is the title of a book by Daniel Tammet

Words For Sounds

give me words for sounds
so I can tell you what I hear

when I say fudda fudda fudda
do you hear a bird flapping its wings?

when I say pft pft pft
do you hear sneakers treading on a concrete path?

when I say sssspe ssssspe ssssspe
do you hear the moorhen whistling in the reeds?

when I say errrr errrr errr
do you hear the toddler in the pram
grizzling on a hot autumn day?

when I say woooo woooo woooo
do you hear the wind blowing in your ear?

give me words for sounds
so I can tell you what I hear
and you can hear with me too

Hear

when the wind blows through the trees
ffffff ffffff
do you hear the sound of leaves rustling in the wind
or do you hear the trees talking to the birds?

when the sea leaps against the shore
ckhrrr ckhrrrr
do you hear the sound of water crushing sand
or do you hear sorrow crashing on the rocks?

when the rain falls on the ground
plop plop
do you hear the sound of water on soil
or do you hear hope blossoming
a flower?

II

Adagio

Searching

when my daughter was born
I lost myself in her eyes
even though they were blue instead of brown
I found myself stroking her hair
even though it was blonde instead of black

lost and found
I spent years sleep-deprived and breastfeeding
changing nappies and keeping watch

when her little sister the bambino was born
I was lost all over again
although this time the blue eyes and blonde hair
weren't as much of a shock
'she looks just like her sister' I said in surprise
when I first gazed in her eyes

and now they are growing
and I'm struggling to find who I am
when the tsunami of childhood is over
to find what it tastes like when I eat my own desires
to find my voice without theirs in my head
to find myself
without them

Wonder

she's walking along the footpath staring intently at her feet
hand clasped in mine
I'm striding ahead, head full of my list of things to do
dragging her along in my wake

she tugs on my hand
'look mama!'
hurriedly I look down at the path to where she is pointing
'It's just a snail' I reply dismissively

and I miss the wonder in her eyes
when she gazes at the thing
the thing with a bright shiny silver trail glistening
glistening behind it mama
as it slowly inches along the path

Mother

keep her secret heart
close and deep
a rushing river
savage, tender
– awe

Tender

she's snuggled deep into the hollow of my belly
her back pressed firmly against my front

her head is lying on my outstretched arm
the warm soles of her small feet rest on my thighs

my nose is pressed into the hair on the back of her head
it tickles as I breathe in her soft sunshiny scent

my other arm encircles the tender flesh of her abdomen
her arm pins it in place

I lie awake in the pale morning light
feeling her chest
rise and fall
rise and fall
rise and fall

outside the currawong calls

Fierce

when she was little
she would sing herself to sleep
strapped in her car seat
as we drove and drove and drove

now her fists pummel
me in fury
when I tell her
'no'

Daylight Savings

salty kisses
mermaid wishes
sparkling fishes
screw the dishes

Afternoons

she's sitting sideways on the couch
underneath the west facing window
her bare feet are tucked close to her bottom
and her back is pressed against the arm rest

propped on her knees is a book
in her lap, a ceramic bowl filled with salami

she sits and reads and chews and reads
outside the wind blows through palm leaves
and grey clouds gather a darkening sky

My Time

I'm lying in bed, trying to turn off my brain and nap
up since 3 a.m. after the damn cat woke me
chomping kibble at the end of my bed
crunch crunch crunch
and I couldn't get back to sleep

as I lie, brain buzzing
the door opens and closes softly
the covers are thrown off
and she climbs on my head
to lie on the other side of me

'fine' I say
'you can be here but don't make a sound'
and I pull the covers back over my body

she's quiet
but keeps tossing and turning
to get my attention
'stop that' I grunt and grump
eyes shut, determined denial

the more I groan
the more she fidgets
ants in her pants

until I surrender
gather her into my arms
snuggle her in tight
lips on soft cheek
heart filled with tender
and she is still

Dinner Time

the oil sizzles in the pan
and the smell of frying onions
steals into the room

at the kitchen table
two girls sit and fold
coloured origami squares
into cunning paper foxes

I turn on the fan
when I add the meat
stirring quickly so it doesn't burn

faces appear on the foxes
eyelashes, lipstick and berets
necklaces, high heels and handbags
names are given and personalities created
lovers are married and children born

turning down the heat
I sprinkle herbs and salt into the pan
and add a tin of tomatoes

'can I be your BFF?' asks Saffron
'Andromeda Blossom's already my BFF' says Coco
'oh.'
'you can be my second-best BFF.'
'goody! I'm going to tell Mummy.
Mummy, I'm Coco's second-best BFF!'

Bedtime

it's at bedtime
when the invitation comes
to throw off the day's drudgery
and indulge in joy and glee and mischief

it's at bedtime
when I am so tired
I can barely think
and all I can think about
is getting the kids in bed

they skip and play
make cheeky remarks
find bright and shiny things
jump out of their skins

'get your pjs on,' I bark quickly
as I grab the laundry basket to put on a load of washing
while they decide now is the time to write a letter to their best friend

'brush your teeth,' I yell
from the kitchen while I wash the dishes and wipe down the table
knowing they're playing with their toys instead

'why haven't you brushed your hair yet?' I snap
as I come into their bedroom to find
they've constructed a fort made of pillows and blankets
and are hiding inside, giggling and waiting to be found

'what do you mean you need to go to the toilet?
I thought you went 10 minutes ago?' I groan
as I choose a book from the shelf for a bedtime story
while they practise headstands against the wall

until
their joy and my fatigue
collide
in a screaming match and tears
slamming doors and hurtful words
broken hearts and regretful mamas

A Friend of Mine

joy popped round last week
unannounced
for a brief visit

I was rushing around the house
in my trackky dacks
putting away the groceries
getting dinner on and washing the dishes
if I'd have known she was popping in
I would have brushed my hair
put on some glitter and a clean pair of jeans

she stayed long enough to share
the beauty and wonder
of my daughters' imaginary play
just as I was beginning to see
she left
as quickly as she came

III

Variation A

Burn

the blood, the blood
runs deep
they say

the earth, the earth
stands firm

the air, the air
smells sweet
they say

the earth, the earth
stands firm

the tears the tears
heal all
they say

my soul
        my soul
                still burns

Ignite

I've got a hunger
gnawing holes
in my belly

I've got a fire
burning pain
in my soul

I've got a thirst
raining desire
in my heart

I'm out of control

Write Me a Poem

I want to pin sounds
of birds, insects, wind and rain
on a page
a botanist
piercing a butterfly

I want to capture emotions
of joy, hope, lust and rage
in a portrait
a photographer
with a zoom lens

I want to dissect motives
of politicians, mothers and lawyers
in a phrase
a surgeon
wielding a scalpel

give me the sharp mind
the steady hand
the true ear
and the poet's wit

My Words

I want words
my words
to sing and dance
off the page

I want words
my words
to sing and dance
in your ear

words like synesthesia
and cumquat
– marmalade for the soul

I want words words words
words to sing
and words to dance
words to whisper
and to shout
words to wound
and words to heal

I want words
my words
to sing and dance
off the page

I want words
my words
to sing and dance
in your ear

words like defenestration
and visceral
– daggers for the mind

I want words
my words
to sing and dance
so you hear

No thing

Nothing
no thing

not hing
not (h) in g(ood)
nothing

n
o
    thing
          o
          o
          d

Waterfall

when I think
about my inadequate words
and how they fail to describe my emotions

when I think
about how much I want to write
beautiful words to sing and dance

tears fall down my cheeks, a waterfall
unending
a quiet stream of sorrow
(yep, I told you. terrible, I know)

but I can't be self-indulgent and cry all day
I'm the one holding it all together
and there's work to do
I've got to wash the dishes
water the plants
feed the cat
make the beds
sweep the floor
and pay the bills

so I shout at the kids instead

Failure

what do you do
when you discover
you're no good at doing
the thing you love most of all?

Do you

a) pretend it's not your fault everyone else has more time, talent and money than you?

b) attend a class and earnestly take notes in the hope some of it will rub off on you?

c) curl up in a ball in the corner and hope to die?

Empty

Praise me – I command you
sing glories of me to all the Gods in the heavens
Artemis, Indra and Ra
while you shower me with glitter and confetti
until I glow golden like Oscar
clutched in a starlet's hand

Adore me – I implore you
fall at my feet and shower my path
with rose petals grown on the Ecuadorian equator
while you strum your 15-stringed lute
and sing sonnets of my incandescent beauty
under the light of the quickening moon

Worship me – I demand you
kneel at my shrine with offerings
of freshly baked bread and sweet golden wine
while you sit with head bowed
and wait patiently for words of jewelled wisdom
to fall from my perfectly formed lips

Fill me – I beg of you
grab a wooden bucket
and pour into it with a generous hand
lavish compliments and extravagant accolades
to fill the voracious void of despair and longing
masquerading as my soul

Screw It

screw it
just screw it
rhyme, metre and iambic pentameter
screw the whole friggin' lot

who cares about Petrarchan sonnets
and imperfect rhymes?
seriously
who
            the
                        hell
                                    cares?

screw it

just write it down

Instructions For Poets

how to write a poem
1. take a knife
2. slice open your wrist
3. pour the words on to the page

how to recite a poem
1. rip open your shirt
2. bare your soul
3. die a thousand deaths

how to receive feedback
1. steel yourself
2. take everything personally
3. curl in the foetal position

Soul Ink

I scratch my soul
in lines of ink upon the page
tracing my journey
into the heart of darkness
charting foreign lands
and impossible beasts
drawn in the corners
deep soul diving into
the truth of my life
as it is right now
or perhaps yesterday
because we all like to live in the past

The Shift

there's this thing
it happens in brilliant poems
where you're listening
or reading the words
swept up in the imagery
of a slide curving and swerving
from the top of a treehouse
to the bottom
when suddenly
on the way down
the slide
turns into someone's insides
and you're running your fingers
along the walls of her womb

The Poet's Express

there's a freight train running through my head
spewing complete sentences and ideas on the track
stopping at no stations
taking no passengers

and I've no paper
or pen
to pin those words to the page
what kind of a poet am I?

Neo Logo

they come in a wave
crash on the shores
one after the other
after the other
after the other
a steady steam
a ready-made poem
a gift

Twenty Years

it's been twenty years
twenty years
since I sat on a blue sheepskin rug
on the cold front porch
of my outer suburban Canberra share house

twenty years since I sat smoking cigarettes
then stubbing them out in a jar before screwing the lid back on
to write another line of angst ridden poetry
all heartbreak and tears
scars earned battles lost

and now?

now

twenty years later
the hunger is back
the words are ripping through my brain
a roaring freight train
twenty years of ideas
barrelling down the track

I don't write with pen and paper no more
I don't even live in outer suburban Canberra
now when the words tear through my head
I whip out my phone instead
thumbs tapping madly
three bajillion spelling errors and typos later
as frantically I keep up with the rushing tide

of twenty years

The Problem

I've got this idea for a poem
it's rather clever I think
the only problem is
I can't figure out how to end it
or what I'm trying to say
really, the clever idea
is just some pretty words
– a thought or similar two

it's the problem with most
of my poems I know
they have no purpose
only a beautiful, shining idea
soul bright, glistening night
sharp and bold

Green Grass

why are the poems
I admire the most
the ones
least like mine?

mine are sparse
brief
brutal

those others?
passionate, lengthy epics
a journey of fire

mine are plain
ordinary
naked

those others?
lyrical prose dancing on graves
in storms of desire

still I write
whittled to bone
my naked, brutal lines

Blue

I can't explain blue to you
well, I could
it's a colour
fifth on the spectrum
(of light)
it's midnight cold
summer sky

but the point
– what was the point again?
oh yes
I can't explain my blue
butterfly ocean
eight bar
cold toes
blue
to you

I can describe it
and you can imagine
you know what I mean
and I can think you understand
but I'll never know
if you see
the same blue
as me

Lies

I've been telling myself lies again

I always write about myself
and not social issues
my poetry is deeply personal
first person perspective
lies

oh I don't use adjectives
or big words
my poems are humble
and poor
lies

I don't know how to end poems
I said to myself
late one night as I was falling asleep
lies

a quick trip yesterday
in my blue phone box tardis
back through space and time
to the not so distant past
of my first (and only) published book of poetry
and I found it was lies
all lies

there are beautiful adjectives
deeply moving accounts
portraits of other people
ruminations on social issues
universal truths
and incredible endings

oh memory, you false and fatal friend
you've failed me yet again

But What Does It Mean?

I don't know

sometimes the words sound pretty
when I put them together

sometimes they rhyme
side by side

sometimes the rhythm
pounds and swirls

and sometimes
I capture something so big
and so true
I don't want to look too close
or scare away the magic
I just want to hint
at the mystery
hunter green
barefoot sky
still and deep

This

there's this moment
when I unfurl
my story to you
in a few brief lines on the page

and into those lines
you breathe life
and whole worlds
spinning through black holes
and into dark matter

you see hope and despair
connections and meaning
I never saw there

and in this moment
of revelation
the story is gone
no longer mine
it is yours

Schroedinger

there's a cat in a box
or maybe not
maybe it's alive
or maybe not

the idea of the cat
of life of death
ripe fruit bulging
taste buds salivating
nostrils flaring
fruit withering
mouth drying
hope dying
the shape of things to come
or not

cat? what cat?
she says
when she opens the box

It's All Been Done

there are no new ideas under the sun
it's all old and been done

what a depressing thought
if I believed it
I'd never write another line

and yet I just found out
my latest clever idea
of a dedication to my reader
has already been done
(of course it's already been done
there are no new ideas under the sun)

Fear

what if this is it?
what if I never write another poem?
what if the ideas flee
the words fail me
and I am done
all poetry gone
what then?

Muse

too soon in a poker game
with the goddess of fate
I reveal my hand to you
now she mocks and spurns
shuns by turns
the muse fled
my art dead

Directions to the Edge

I'll find my edge
out beyond the plains of possibility
turn left at the realms of reality
then on through the isles of insanity

meet me there?

IV

Variation B

Your Turn

now it's time
for your words
to dance with
my thoughts
upon the following pages

Tell Me

what do you think
when you read these words:

'turn the world around'

What Do You Feel

when I say,

'fold time into your future self'

And What Do You Hear

when you read,

'a melody of night sky'

Most Importantly

what do *you* want?
(go on
write it down
we're all friends here)

V

Coda

The Trick Is

the trick is this

write what you need to write
right now

write what you want to write
right now

write what you know to be true
right now

but! (there's always a but...)

do not
I repeat
do not
tell yourself a story about your writing

do not
tell yourself what you can and can't do

just
    write
        down
            the
                words

Stop Apologising

stop apologising
for every breath you take
stand
tall and proud

quit cowering
in the corner of life
sing
out loud

cease hiding
all your gifts
love
true and deep

stop playing small
so you can fit in
dance
wild and free

shine your incredible light
to the world
laugh
raucous and bold

speak your truth
claim your space
you belong

Seekers of the Edge

find the place
where you feel most uncomfortable
and inch your way out
on that limb

gulp as you stare
at the impossible drop below
and wonder how
you'll ever get down safely

throw safety out the window
as you leap from the branch
find you've grown feathers
and fly

You've Got This

you don't need a book
to tell you what to do
you already know

you don't need a class
to tell you what to do
you already know

you don't need a guru
to tell you what to do
you already know

you already know
everything you need to know
you've just forgotten it
now it's time to remember

you've got this
you know what to do
go do it

Run On

eat the animals
rend the flesh
fierce hunter
run on

sing the pain
tell the truth
storyteller
run on

bend the line
feel the pause
sensitive reader
run on

Acknowledgements

Thank you to creative writing teacher Megan Waters for reintroducing me to poetry. I can't believe it was almost twenty years between poems!

Big thanks to Judith Rodriguez for her wonderful poetry class at CAE (she was the amazing lecturer I always dreamt I would have at university) and for creating a monthly poetry group.

Shout-out to all my fellow poets at Moat Poets. You inspire me each month with your generosity, words and stories. Thank you for listening to mine.

I owe a debt to writing buddies Sharon Herbert and Nuwan Wellalage for all their support and suggestions. And also to Jacqui Grace for teaching my girls while I wrote poetry.

Thank you to Michelle McCowage whose brilliant poem inspired my poem 'The Shift'.

Much gratitude to Hadas Schwartzbord for her open- armed welcome and fascinating stories. With your tales and passion, you reminded me of the power of words and the importance of all our stories.

Mel Turnbull – big love for all your awesome nature connection work and introducing me to fox walking, owl eyes and kangaroo ears.

To Meli de Groot, Kate Horne and Amy Kirkup for listening, always. Catriona Bryce, oldest friend, thanks for cheering me on and believing in my poetry. I promise I'll sign this one for you.

Many thanks to my publisher, Stephen Matthews for publishing a young unknown poet all those years ago and making my dream of being a published author come true. Thank you for believing in my work and waiting so patiently for the second collection.

Much love to my beautiful girls Airlie and Phoebe for their encouragement and kind words when I read out these poems as I was writing them. They're the best cheer squad ever.

To Gareth – what can I say except the old cliché? Without you, none of this would have been possible. Thank you.

www.ingramcontent.com/pod-product-compliance
Lightning Source LLC
Chambersburg PA
CBHW072207100526
44589CB00015B/2408

* 9 7 8 1 7 6 0 4 1 8 3 2 8 *